# The Chinese Language for Beginners

# The
# Chinese Language
## for Beginners

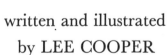

written and illustrated
by LEE COOPER

## CHARLES E. TUTTLE COMPANY
Rutland, Vermont & Tokyo, Japan

T 90518

495. 1

*Representatives*        Cooper

*For the British Isles & Continental Europe:*
SIMON & SCHUSTER INTERNATIONAL GROUP, *London*

*For Australasia:*
BOOKWISE INTERNATIONAL
*1 Jeanes Street, Beverley, 5009, South Australia*

1. Chinese Languages

Published by the Charles E. Tuttle Company, Inc.
of Rutland, Vermont & Tokyo, Japan
with editorial offices at
Suido 1-chome, 2–6, Bunkyo-ku, Tokyo

Library of Congress Catalog Card No. 70–151121
International Standard Book No. 0–8048–0918–6

First printing, 1971
Thirteenth printing, 1988


PRINTED IN JAPAN

*To*
Diane Montllor
*this book is fondly dedicated*

Grateful recognition is given to

Dr. Robert H. Shaw

*Professor, Mary Washington College*

for his help in preparing the manuscript for this book. The author deeply appreciates his thoughtful criticisms, his invaluable suggestions, his constant encouragement.

The Chinese language has no
alphabet. The writing is made
up of simple drawings called
characters.

 *rén*

This sketch of a two-legged creature means **man**. The character for man is used in many words.

A man holding his arms outstretched means **is big** or simply **big**:  *dà*

An extra dot on the "big" character means **too** or **too much**:  *tai*

 *yī*

This character means **one** or **level**.

The level on which things grow:
**the earth**

土 *tŭ*

Two men sitting on the earth:
**sit, sits**

坐 *dzò*

Something under the level:
**down**

下 *shià*

Something above the level:
**up, on**

上 *shang̀*

Each character is pronounced as a one-syllable word. A word usually has one of these four tones:

high,        rising,        dipping,        falling

These tones are shown on pronunciation syllables by these marks:

    —  high (example: *yī*)
    &#47;  rising (example: *rén*)
    &#8995;  dipping (example: *tŭ*)
    &#65340;  falling (example: *dà*)

        *      *      *

In a compound word, the second syllable frequently loses its tone mark as in *péng yu*.

Each syllable contains at least one vowel. The sounds of the vowels are:

**a** as *a* in *father* (example: *dà*)
**ai** as *ai* in *aisle* (example: *taì*)
**e** as *u* in *us* (example: *reń*)
**ei** as *ei* in *reign* (example: *dzeí*)
**i** as *i* in *machine* (example: *yī*)
**o** as *o* in *so* (example: *dzò*)
**u** as *u* in *rule* (example: *tǔ*)
**ü** as *u* in *amusing* (example: *yǜ*)

Now you are ready to read a short story in Chinese!

You will notice that the little words we use in practically every English sentence, *a*, *an*, and *the*, are not used at all in the Chinese language.

And you start at the top of a sentence

and

read

down

!

*Reń dà.*   The man is big.

大人坐下

*Dà reń dzò shià*.　The big man sits down.

*Reń taì dà!*  The man is too big!

One side of this character has the shape of a new moon. So the character means **moon**:

月 *yüeh*

A hand 尹 pointing to the moon 月, **have, has**:

有 *yǔ*

A hand 尹 pointing to the earth 土, **is on, are on**:

在 *dzaì*

人在月上

*Reń dzaì yüeh shang̀.*   A man is on the moon.

Sometimes two characters are required
for one meaning, for example the word
**friend**.

The first character is a moon and his
companion:

朋 *peng*

The second is the left hand ナ
pointing to the right hand 又:

友 *yu*

*Reń yŭ peń yu.* The man has a friend.

Three mountain peaks: **mountain**　　山　*shān*

Two horns on an animal: **sheep**　　羊　*yáng*

Just as the word sheep can refer to one sheep or several sheep, Chinese uses the same characters for both singular and plural. So the sentence below can mean:

"A sheep is on a mountain." or
"Some sheep are on some mountains."

羊在山上

*Yáng dzaì shān shang.* A sheep is on a mountain.

*bū*

This character means **no** or **not**. It is used in a negative sentence and in a question:

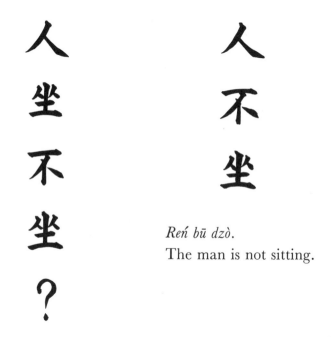

*Reń dzò bū dzò?*
Is the man sitting?

*Reń bū dzò.*
The man is not sitting.

To answer *"yes"* to "Is the man sitting?", repeat the *positive* part of the sentence:

*Reń dzò.*
The man is sitting.

To answer *"no"* to "Is the man sitting?", repeat the *negative* part of the sentence:

*Reń bū dzò.*
The man is not sitting.

 *kŏ*

This character means **mouth**, so it is used in words having to do with the use of the mouth. For example, **bite**:

咬 *yaŏ*

When a person talks, he uses his mouth to *speak* a *language*, so both of these characters must be used to mean **talk**:

**speak** 說 *shō*

**language** 話 *huà*

The mouth character is also used to indicate that a word sounds like another word. The word **and**, 和 *hé,* for instance, sounds like the word for growing grain 禾 *hé*:

**and**  *hé*

 *shr̀*

This character is used between two nouns to mean **is** or **are**.

人
是
朋
友

*Reń shr̀ peńg yu*. The man is a friend.

Some pages of the
next story will
have more than one
line of Chinese.

Read first the line

reading 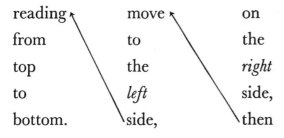 move on

from to the

top the *right*

to *left* side,

bottom. side, then

人有朋友
人說話

*Reń yǔ peń yu*.　The man has a friend.
*Reń shō huà*.　The man talks.

朋友不說話
朋友是羊

*Penǵ yu bū shō huà.* The friend does not speak.
*Penǵ yu shr̀ yanǵ!* The friend is a sheep!

A hand 手 held near an eye 目 means look at: 看 *kàn*

A man with one huge eye means to see: 見 *jièn*

Since one must *look at* something in order *to see* it, both of these characters must be used to mean **see**.

人看見山

*Reń kàn jièn shañ.*   The man sees a mountain.

At one time shells were used as money in China. So a shell 貝 next to a weapon 戎 means **thief**: A thief is always grabbing things. The word **grab** is made up of two characters: the first is a big 大 bird 隹 only an inch 寸 away from being grabbed by an enemy; the other is the ear 耳 of a captured animal, grabbed by a hunter's right hand 又 :

賊 *dzeí*

奪 *dě*

取 *chǚ*

賊奪取羊

*Dzeí dě chǚ yang.*   The thief grabs the sheep.

The one 一 who rules over the earth
土 is of course a **king**:

王 *wang̓*

The king's favorite ornaments are made of **jade**:

玉 *yǜ*

玉 *yǜ*
的 *de*
} **made of jade**

A dragon's tail 乚 is the natural ending for the character meaning **dragon**:

龍 *lung̓*

A pig 豕 with a big head and ivory tusks forms the character for **elephant**:

象 *shiang̀*

An animal 犭 running from another animal with an open mouth 句 means **dog**:

狗 *goǔ*

**China** was once the center of the civilized world. So the Chinese call their land:

**center** 中 *juńg*

**country** 國 *gue*

The Chinese call the **United States of America**:

**beautiful** 美 *meĭ*

**country** 國 *gue*

*Juńg gue reń hé Meĭ gue reń shr̀ peńg yu.*
The Chinese and the American are friends.

國王有龍、象、狗、

*Gué wanǵ yǔ lunǵ, shiang̀, goǔ.*
The king has a dragon, an elephant, a dog.

賊奪取龍

龍是玉的

*Dzeí dě chǚ lung̈.*   A thief grabs the dragon.
*Lung̈ shr̀ yǜ de.*   The dragon is made of jade.

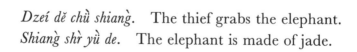

賊奪取象
象是玉的

*Dzeí dĕ chǔ shiang̀.*  The thief grabs the elephant.
*Shiang̀ shr̀ yù de.*  The elephant is made of jade.

賊奪取王
王是玉的

*Dzeí dĕ chǜ waṅ́.*   The thief grabs the king.
*Waṅ́ shr̀ yǜ de.*   The king is made of jade.

狗不是玉的
狗咬賊

*Goŭ bū shr̀ yù de*.　The dog is not made of jade.
*Goŭ yaŏ dzeí!*　The dog bites the thief!

# VOCABULARY

This vocabulary list contains all the Chinese characters used in the book, arranged in the order in which they appear.

| CHARACTER | PRONUNCIATION | MEANING |
|---|---|---|
| 人 | *reń* | man |
| 大 | *dà* | big; is big |
| 太 | *tai* | too; too much |
| 一 | *yī* | one; level |
| 土 | *tŭ* | earth |
| 坐 | *dzò* | sit |
| 下 | *shià* | down |
| 上 | *shang̀* | up; on |
| 月 | *yüeh̀* | moon |
| 有 | *yŭ* | have, has |
| 在 | *dzai* | is on, are on |

| CHARACTER | PRONUNCIATION | MEANING |
|-----------|---------------|---------|
| 朋 | *peng̅* ⎫ | friend |
| 友 | *yu* ⎭ | |
| 山 | *shan̄* | mountain |
| 羊 | *yang̅* | sheep |
| 不 | *bū* | no, not |
| 口 | *kǒ* | mouth |
| 咬 | *yaǒ* | bite |
| 説 | *shō* ⎫ speak | speaks |
| 話 | *huà* ⎭ | language |
| 和 | *hé* | and |
| 是 | *shr̀* | is, are |
| 看 | *kaǹ* ⎫ see | look at |
| 見 | *jieǹ* ⎭ | see |
| 賊 | *dzeí* | thief |

| CHARACTER | PRONUNCIATION | MEANING |
|---|---|---|
| 奪取 | *dě* / *chǔ* | grab |
| 王 | *wáng* | king |
| 玉 | *yǜ* | jade |
| 玉的 | *yǜ* / *de* | made of jade |
| 龍 | *lúng* | dragon |
| 象 | *shiàng* | elephant |
| 狗 | *goǔ* | dog |
| 中國 | *jūng* / *gue* | center / country — China, Chinese |
| 美國 | *meǐ* / *gue* | beautiful / country — U.S.A. |
| 國 | *gué* | country |